THE HISTORY OF EXPLORATION
Pioneers of the

AIR

New
Forest
Press

Publisher: Tim Cook
Editor: Guy Croton
Designer: Carol Davis
Production Controller: Ed Green
Production Manager: Suzy Kelly

ISBN: 978-1-84898-306-9
Library of Congress Control Number: 2010925464
Tracking number: nfp0003

U.S. publication © 2010 New Forest Press
Published in arrangement with Black Rabbit Books

PO Box 784, Mankato, MN 56002
www.newforestpress.com

Printed in the USA
9 8 7 6 5 4 3 2 1

Every effort has been made to trace the copyright holders, and we apologize in advance for any omissions. We would
be pleased to insert the appropriate acknowledgments in any subsequent edition of this publication.

The author has asserted her right to be identified as the author of this book in
accordance with the Copyright, Design, and Patents Act, 1988.

CONTENTS

THE DREAM OF FLIGHT

THE MODERN AIR TRAVELER

Today, the modern traveler can feel comfortable in the knowledge that the airplane they board will take them to their planned destination, along a known route, and will remain constantly in touch with the rest of the world. For the early pioneers it was a flight into the unknown. They were flying in untested aircraft, with little means of navigation, unsure if they would live to see where they had landed.

Most people today take flying, air travel, and speed for granted. It is difficult to imagine the bravery, inventiveness, and sometimes sheer genius of the first flying pioneers. Every challenge and every achievement was greeted with incredulity and public acclaim, from the first balloon flight in 1783 to the first successful piloted flight by the Wright brothers in 1903. Flying like the birds was a dream. When people fantasized about flying to the U.S.A. or sending a man to the Moon, they never thought that both would become a reality. In the early years of flight pioneering, many attempts were made to imitate birds, but the 1800s saw two developments that formed the basis of flying and aircraft—the science of flight and the emergence of people who were prepared to experiment with, make, develop, test, and pilot the first flying machines. These were the pioneers of the air.

FLIGHT OF THE GODS

Ancient cultures had legends about flying, but the ability to do so was generally reserved for the gods. In Greek mythology, Daedalus and his son Icarus built wings to allow them to fly. However, ignoring his father's warnings, Icarus flew too close to the Sun and the wax that held the feathers together melted and he fell to his death.

ART & AERONAUTICS

The 15th-century artist Leonardo da Vinci showed a remarkable knowledge of aeronautics well ahead of his time. He studied birds in flight and made sketches of a man-powered flying machine as early as 1500. This model of his flapping-wing machine shows that da Vinci was unable to unlock the secret of enabling humana to fly—it would have required super-human stamina and endurance to keep the craft in the air.

THE BIRDMEN

There are more than 50 documented instances of people trying to fly before 1880. Le Besnier *(below)* was a French locksmith who was reported to have "flown" several feet with the aid of a pair of wood and tafetta wings. The Englishman Thomas Pelling became a local celebrity as a birdman, but he met an untimely end when he jumped from a church tower: the rope broke, and he fell to his death. Viennese watchmaker Jacob Degen *(left)* devised one of the more bizarre early flying machines around 1811. His flapping-wing aircraft, or *ornithopter*, had two flaps that were fastened to his back by a yoke. He moved them up and down with levers worked by his hands and feet. It is not known how far the machine took him, if indeed it ever got off the ground!

Up, Up, & Away

By the late 1700s, it was well known that objects that were lighter than air would rise, but the real pioneers of this knowledge were the brothers Joseph and Etienne Montgolfier. Working in their father's paper factory in southeast France, they noticed how paper would be lifted up the chimney when it was put on the fire. They started to experiment and became convinced that a large bag filled with hot air would rise. The two brothers burned a mixture of wool and straw, which produced what they thought was a "new" gas. After conducting trials with models, they built a large linen bag covered with stiff paper and fastened with buttons, creating the first hot-air balloon. The Montgolfier brothers refused to believe that it was just hot air that made their balloon rise and not their special "Montgolfier gas." Nevertheless, it was due to them that the first human being, Jean François Pilâtre de Rosier, rose from the ground in a tethered balloon.

FRANCESCO DE LANA

The 1600s and 1700s also saw some highly impractical schemes to get airborne. In 1670, Francesco de Lana, a Jesuit priest, suggested a design for an aerial ship suspended by four copper spheres emptied of air. Unfortunately, he overlooked the fact that the atmospheric pressure would have collapsed the spheres.

FLYING HIGH

The first living creatures to fly in free flight were three animals; a sheep, a duck, and a cockerel. They flew in a wicker basket suspended from a balloon on September 19, 1783; a balloon designed by the Montgolfier brothers.

MONTGOLFIER ASCENT

On November 21, 1783, before an amazed Parisian crowd, Jean François Pilâtre de Rosier, accompanied by the Marquis d'Arlandes, took off in a Montgolfier balloon. They flew in free flight over the city for 23 minutes, landing 10 mi. (16km) away. This flight is acknowledged as the first time a man actually flew.

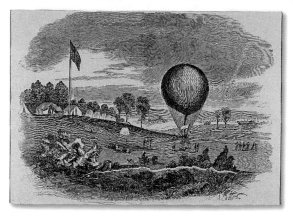

BALLOONS IN WARFARE

One of the more practical uses of balloons was in warfare. Thaddeus Lowe constructed four balloons for the Union Army in Virginia in 1862. They were used during the American Civil War for observation purposes.

JACQUES CHARLES
(1746–1823)

As the Montgolfier brothers were testing their balloon, the French physicist Professor Jacques Charles was building a balloon made of varnished silk, which he filled with hydrogen, known to be 14 times lighter than air. The unmanned balloon was released in Paris, France in August 1783, rose into the air, and was carried 15 mi. (24km) to the village of Gonesse. The peasants thought that they were being attacked by a monster from the sky and destroyed the balloon with sticks and pitchforks. Charles had better luck with his next hydrogen-filled balloon. Accompanied by his assistant Nicolas Robert, the *Charlière* (as hydrogen balloons became known) set off from the Tuileries Gardens in Paris, watched by a crowd of 200,000 people. It traveled 29 mi. (46.5km).

BALLOON RACES

Ballooning developed quickly, following the success of the Montgolfier brothers. Balloon racing became a popular sport with the development of the hydrogen-filled balloon, as can be seen here in Germany in 1908. But ballooning had its limitations—steering was completely dependent on the direction of the wind, and the material used was flammable and susceptible to punctures.

EARLY AIRCRAFT

ALBERTO SANTOS-DUMONT

Ballooning was popular in the 1800s, but others were turning their attention to controllable flight. The major problem for lighter-than-air craft was the failure to find a lightweight source of power. In August 1884, Charles Renard and Arthur Krebs, officers of the French Corps of Engineers, flew the first controllable and powered airship (or dirigible, as airships were then known). Others were looking to develop heavier-than-air craft, and it was the kite, first flown by the Chinese more than 2,000 years ago, that became the inspiration for many inventors. Sir George Cayley used the idea of a kite to discover the basic aeronautical principles. He built the first successful airplane—admittedly, a model glider—but it actually flew! It fell to an Australian, Lawrence Hargrave, to build the box kite that was the key to successful flight and aeronautical design.

In 1852, a small steam engine was attached to a sausage-shaped balloon, and the airship was created. In 1901, the eccentric Brazilian Alberto Santos-Dumont flew his airship around the Eiffel Tower in Paris, France, causing much excitement among the crowds. It was a feat that won him the first prize ever given for aerial achievement. Santos-Dumont used his airships like taxis, often dropping in on friends and leaving his airship tied to their houses. He went on to build a box kite biplane in which he made the first officially observed flight in Europe in 1906. Santos-Dumont was very popular with the French people, not so much for his flying successes as for his many crashes.

OTTO LILIENTHAL (1849–1896)

German Otto Lilienthal was the first to build and fly a glider capable of carrying a person. Lilienthal made more than 2,500 flights, gradually improving his design until he was gliding almost a quarter of a mile (0.5km). He relied on the movement of his body to control the aircraft, but in 1896, he lost control and the glider crashed, killing him. His last words were "Sacrifices must be made," reflecting the true spirit of these early pioneers.

SIR GEORGE CAYLEY (1773–1857)

Sir George Cayley is credited with several scientific principles and inventions, but it is in the field of aeronautics that he made his mark. Known as both the "Father of Aerial Navigation" and the "Father of Flight," Cayley had a huge influence on the development of flight as he recognized the necessity of a scientific approach. In 1804, he built a glider that was strong enough to carry his gardener boy several feet. A later, stronger, model carried his coachman across a narrow valley. On landing, the coachman immediately handed Cayley his letter of resignation!

AERIAL STEAM CARRIAGE

The English engineer William Samuel Henson was a great admirer of George Cayley's work and studied his principles. In 1842, he filed a patent for the Aerial Steam Carriage—the first design for a completely mechanically powered aircraft that actually looked like an airplane. It had two propellers that were driven by a steam engine. A model was built in 1847, but the weight of the engine forced the plane to glide downward.

LANGLEY'S AIRDROME

Dr. Samuel Pierpont Langley was a highly-respected American scientist who designed several tandem-winged planes, one of which was steam-driven. He received a government grant to make a full-size aircraft called the Aerodrome, which was gasoline-driven. The first piloted test flight was in 1903, when it was launched by catapult from the roof of a houseboat on the Potomac River on the East Coast. The launching mechanism failed, and the plane plunged into the river, nearly drowning the pilot. Disappointed and out of funds, Langley gave up the challenge to fly.

THE BOX KITE

Lawrence Hargrave (1850–1915) had little scientific knowledge, but he was a good engineer. He invented the rotary engine in 1887, but it is his invention of the box kite in 1893 that established his place in aviation history. Hargrave demonstrated the lifting power of his box kite when he suspended himself below four kites strung together. He was lifted 16 ft. (5m) into the air. By 1906, most of the first airplanes developed in Europe were designed with wings based on Hargrave's box-kite design.

THE FIRST FLIGHT

Only five people witnessed the world's first powered flight. The scene was set on sand dunes outside Kitty Hawk, North Carolina. This peninsula was chosen because of the strong, almost continuous winds. Wilbur Wright had to run alongside, holding the wing of the *Flyer* to balance it on the track. Then Orville Wright took off on his historic flight. The flight lasted 12 seconds and covered a distance of 120 ft. (37m). This is less than the wingspan of a modern airliner, but at the time it represented a new age in technology.

THE BICYCLE MEN

Orville (1871–1948), left, and Wilbur (1867–1912) Wright were enthusiastic experimenters and skilled craftsmen. They were able to think about a machine's requirements, make it, and watch it work! They owned a business manufacturing and repairing bicycles. They were both private men who were diligent and determined, and they deserved their success.

The value of their contribution to flying, besides being the first to fly in a heavier-than-air machine, was the way that they proved the value of a scientific approach rather than the "build it and see" attitude that had prevailed.

ACHIEVING RECOGNITION

Initially, Orville and Wilbur Wright received very little recognition for their success from fellow Americans. For several years after the first flight, people were skeptical about their achievement. Wilbur went to France to demonstrate a later model of their famous *Flyer*. On October 8, 1908, he was ready for his first flight. A large crowd gathered to watch, many expecting the test to be a failure. When Wilbur successfully landed, the crowd went wild with excitement. The next day, all the French newspapers wrote about his achievement.

THE WRIGHT BROTHERS

The excitement and interest in flight was growing to almost great heights at the turn of the 1900s. Both airships and other lighter-than-air machines were flying successfully. A lot of publicity was focused on the engineers and scientists trying to develop the first powered and controllable airplane capable of carrying a man. When the first successful flight was made, it was by someone who had not been in the public eye. It all began in 1878 when two young brothers, Orville and Wilbur Wright, were given a toy helicopter. This, and reading the work of Otto Lilienthal, spurred them to actively experiment with flying machines. They succeeded in building and piloting one of the largest gliders ever built. They built their own wind tunnel to aid their experiments and also built a small, 12-horsepower gasoline engine to power the craft. Then, on December 17, 1903, they traveled with their newly designed plane, *Flyer*, to the Kill Devil Hill sand dunes in Kitty Hawk. The rest is history.

BODYWORK

This model shows how Orville Wright operated the controls of the *Flyer*. He had to lie face down on the lower wing, left of center, to counterbalance the weight of the engine. He operated the elevator control lever with his hand and the other controls with his hips.

TELEGRAM!

The Wright brothers made four successful flights at Kitty Hawk. Orville sent a telegram to their father announcing their victory and asked him to inform the press. Remarkably, the press reaction was lukewarm, not helped by the fact that the telegraph operator had mistakenly put that the duration of the flight was 57 seconds. The real time of 12 seconds seemed anticlimactic.

SUCCESS AND FAILURE

At first, the U.S. government didn't acknowledge the Wright Brothers' claims that they could fly. While Wilbur was flying in France, Orville was breaking records for endurance in America. Then, on September 17, 1908, mechanical failure caused the *Flyer* to crash. Orville broke his leg, but his passenger, Lieutenant Selfridge, was killed, making him the first victim of an airplane disaster. Not to be deterred, Orville continued and enjoyed success the following year in Berlin, Germany, as can be seen here.

LOUIS BLÉRIOT
& FAMILY

Louis Blériot (1872–1936) had made a fortune and spent most of it on flying. He had a reputation for being enthusiastic about crazy ideas and was seen as something of a joke. He bought several airplanes from the Voissin brothers, and the kindest that can be said of their designs is that many of them were misguided. On one occasion, in a demonstration in Paris, France, a Voissin airplane fell apart before takeoff! But the result of Blériot's cross-Channel flight was remarkable. Blériot amassed another fortune selling hundreds of his planes, but sadly, his flying skills did not improve. After a crash, he had to give up flying, and he died virtually penniless in 1936.

THOSE MAGNIFICENT MEN & THEIR FLYING MACHINES

The first decade of the 1900s saw flying becoming established. The Wright brothers had set the scene, and many others wanted to follow. In the U.S.A., Glenn Curtiss and his associates were actively involved in the Aerial Experiment Association. In France, the Voissin brothers adapted their factory to build airplanes, and enthusiasts followed every development with excitement. Even Santos-Dumont transferred his interest from airships to aircraft, much to the delight of the French crowds, as his "near misses" became even more dramatic. But there were people who mistrusted the idea of flight, and others who discouraged it. In England in 1909, A.V. Roe flew his triplane and was threatened with prosecution for disturbing the peace, but a few days later this was forgotten when the Frenchman Louis Blériot successfully flew across the English Channel. This flight was one of the most important advances in aviation.

CROSSING THE ENGLISH CHANNEL

At the beginning of 1909, the British newspaper, the *Daily Mail* offered a £1,000 ($1,600) prize to anyone who could fly across the Channel. Many tried, including two serious challengers; Count Charles de Lambert, who withdrew after crashing, and Hubert Latham, whose engine failed several miles out to sea, where he sat, smoking a cigar, waiting to be rescued. The disorganized Blériot won the prize on July 25, 1909, when he set off from France in poor visibility with no compass. Finding that he was lost, he followed some fishing boats, guessing that they were heading for Dover, England. When he reached England, he flew along the coastline until he saw a man waving a flag. He crash-landed 37 minutes after leaving France, becoming an instant celebrity.

GLENN CURTISS (1878–1930)

Curtiss was an American pioneer who conducted similar research to the Wright brothers, although he placed his pilots in a sitting position. He made his first public flight in the U.S.A. on March 12, 1908, and in 1909, won the world's first air race in Rheims, France. Local wine growers had organized a Festival of Flying, and there were prize money and trophies to be won. Curtiss won the most prestigious: the Gordon Bennett Cup.

PIONEERS OF THE AIR
-A TIMELINE-

~1896~
Otto Lilienthal dies in glider crash

~1900~
World's first rigid airship built by Count Ferdinand von Zeppelin

~1901~
Alberto Santos-Dumont flies around the Eiffel Tower in his airship

~1903~
Wright Brothers make world's first powered controlled flight by airplane

~1906~
Santos-Dumont makes the first officially observed flight in Europe

~1907~
Paul Cornu designs and builds the first helicopter

~1908~
Flyer crashes, and Lieutenant Selfridge becomes the first air-crash victim

Wilbur Wright achieves recognition in France

Samuel Cody makes the first flight in England

~1909~
Louis Blériot flies across English Channel in 37 minutes

THE DEPERDUSSIN

By 1913, French aviation led the world. The *Deperdussin* was difficult to fly but could reach speeds in excess of 100 mph (160km/h)—the fastest thing in the sky. For more practical use, the seaplane was also being developed, like this Deperdussin Seagull.

TOM SOPWITH (1888–1989)

Tom Sopwith made a memorable debut on the aeronautical scene in 1910, when he crashed his plane at Brooklands, England in an early British air display. The next day he decided to learn to fly! He became a test pilot, set up a flying school, and designed and manufactured many of the aircraft used in World War I.

SAMUEL CODY (1862–1913)

Samuel Franklin Cody was a larger-than-life character who, in 1908, made the first flight in England. He demonstrated the abilities of man-carrying kites with the help of his family—on one occasion, he lifted his wife aloft in a kite and forgot her for several hours! Later, Cody turned his attention to manned flight. The aircraft that he built reflected Cody's character. They were so large that they were known as "Flying Cathedrals."

RACE FOR THE SKIES

The interest in flight had been growing steadily, but Blériot's cross-Channel flight in 1909 caused an unparaleled surge of excitement. The Festival of Flying in Rheims, France was attended by royalty, and people traveled from all over the world to be there. It became an annual event. There were many other awards and prizes, events, and exhibitions, which gave a great boost to the development of the airplane. The Aéro Club of America sponsored events. Prize money was offered for a "Round-Britain" flight. But the most prized in these early days was the Schneider Trophy. It is considered that the races for the Schneider Trophy accelerated progress so much that twenty years of research were condensed into just six. Race winners became heroes.

U.S. AIR RACES

By the 1930s, air races were attracting huge crowds in the United States. The premier race was for the Thompson Trophy. It was open to all aircraft over a course of 50 mi. (80.5km). The first all-women race took place in Cleveland, Ohio in 1929 and became known as the "Powder-Puff Derby." It had 23 competitors, including Amelia Earhart. But other women had already made their mark in aviation history. The French Baroness de Laroche was the first woman to receive a pilot's license by the Aéro Club of France in 1910.

THE SCHNEIDER TROPHY

Jacques Schneider presented this bronze trophy to the Aéro Club of France in 1913. It was originally meant to encourage marine craft, but instead it developed into an air race. The first race was in Monaco in 1913 but was suspended during World War I and restarted in 1919 off the Isle of Wight, U.K. Races continued until 1931, when Great Britain won the trophy outright, having won three consecutive races.

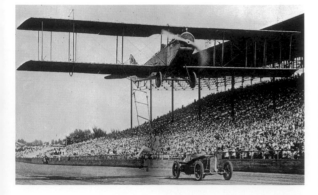

AIR SHOWS

After World War I, many unemployed pilots found work as traveling showmen, entertaining the crowds with aerial tricks such as wing walking. A combined air and car display took place at Brooklands Circuit in England. The circuit had been built for car racing, but it failed to attract good audiences. The central grassed area was used to introduce aviation as an additional attraction.

JIMMY DOOLITTLE

American pioneer Jimmy Doolittle (1896–1993) was better known on the car-racing circuit than in the air. But in 1923, he won the Schneider Trophy in a U.S. Army seaplane *(above)*. He went on to win the first Bendix Trophy and the Thompson Trophy, where he set a new world record speed of 294 mph (473km/h). He also pioneered the use of aeronautical instruments and was the first man to fly "blind" in 1929, guided purely by instruments.

AVIATION MEETS

Aviation meetings were very popular and gave people the opportunity to get close to airplanes. Huge crowds attended most of the air displays.

WINNING THE SCHNEIDER TROPHY

The first winner of the Schneider Trophy was Maurice Prevost. He was the only pilot to complete the course. Tom Sopwith and Harry Hawker brought a Sopwith Tabloid airplane for the 1914 race. It won at an average speed of 86.7 mph (139.5km/h), almost double that of the previous year's winner. The last race of 1931 was won by a Supermarine S 6B at an average speed of 340 mph (547km/h). Like this replica, the high-speed Schneider floatplanes provided the opportunities for developing strong, light, streamlined machines, which pointed the way to the fighters of the future.

PIONEERS OF THE AIR
-A TIMELINE-

~1909~
First aviation exhibition is sponsored by the city of Rheims

Glenn Curtiss wins world's first air race

~1910~
Baroness Raymonde de Laroche becomes the first woman to gain her pilot's license

~1913~
First race takes place for the Schneider Trophy

~1914–18~
World War I produces many flying aces and accelerates developments in aviation

~1917~
William Boeing starts the Boeing Airplane Company

~1919~
Alcock and Brown fly nonstop across the Atlantic Ocean

~1922~
Juan Trippe starts Colonial Air Transport, the forerunner to Pan Am

~1924~
Alan Cobham flies from London, England to Cape Town, South Africa

WORLD WAR I

COUNT ZEPPELIN

This commemorative medal is of Count Ferdinand von Zeppelin, the founder of the company that built the first fleet of Zeppelin airships. They were 420 ft. (128m) long, with a basic design of 16 internal gas cells encased in a shell of aluminum and cotton. They were the largest machines ever to have flown. Before the war, they were used to carry passengers, setting up the first passenger air service. During the war, they were used as bombers.

Few people believed that there was any value to aircraft in wartime, except for reconnaissance. There were some halfhearted experiments at dropping bombs and torpedoes and firing guns from planes, but they weren't taken seriously. When the first allied planes flew out to France in 1914, they didn't carry guns. Their only instructions were to ram any Zeppelin airship that they came across. The Germans had the advantage in the air in the first two years of the war. They used airplanes designed by a young Dutchman, Anthony Fokker. His designs were original and purposeful, and early on in the war, he designed an interruptor gear that allowed a forward-facing gun to be fired through propellers without damaging them. By 1916, the allies, too, were developing airplanes as war machines. A different type of flying was required. The newly trained pilots of World War I were the pioneers of their time—the aces of the air.

LA PUISSA

AMERICA'S ACE

Captain Eddie Rickenbacker was America's most celebrated hero of the First World War. Before the war, he was a top race car driver. When the Americans joined the war in April 1917, Rickenbacker was originally rejected as a pilot, because at the age of 27 he was considered to be too old. He finally managed to join a squadron, but as Colonel Billy Mitchell's driver. It was Colonel Mitchell who arranged for Rickenbacker's pilot training. By the end of the war, Rickenbacker had shot down four balloons and 22 aircraft to become America's top flying ace.

THE ALLIED ATTACKS

The British developed a strategy for combating the German's early superiority in the skies. It was to improve aircraft, train personnel, and take the air war to the Germans—attacking and pursuing them relentlessly. Factories were built, aircraft design and construction became an established business, and planes were rapidly developed. The French supported these plans, and many allied aces made their mark: René Fonck from France, Edward (Micky) Mannock from Great Britain, and William (Billy) Bishop from Canada, to name but a few.

THE FOKKER EINDECKER

Anthony Fokker (1890–1939) had two interests in life, airplanes and money. He admitted that he would sell anything to the first person who showed him the money. The British were not interested in Fokker's designs. It was the Germans who took the initiative, and the *Fokker Eindecker* was in use from the first days of the war. After the war, Fokker returned to his native country of the Netherlands and started his own factory. He was a pioneer of aircraft design developing a series of high-winged monoplanes.

THE RED BARON

Baron Manfred von Richthofen (1882–1918) was a popular hero in Germany. His distinctive red Fokker triplane earned him the nickname the "Red Baron." He received the highest German honor for his service, the *Ordre pour le Merité*, which became known as the Blue Max after Max Immelmann, another flying ace and recipient of the award. Richthofen was credited with shooting down 80 allied planes during World War I before he himself was shot down and killed.

The First Fighters

In 1903 the Wright Brothers made the first successful airplane flights in the U.S.A. Seven years later, the British Secretary of State for War said, *"We do not consider that aeroplanes will be of any possible use for war purposes."* This view was held by officials around the world, including in France which rapidly became the center of aviation pioneering. However, in 1912 the British military formed the Royal Flying Corps (R.F.C.), to fly reconnaissance missions to see what enemy troops were doing. Just for fun, the pilots began firing at kites with rifles and revolvers. By 1913 one of the first military aircraft was put on display by the giant Vickers company. Called the "Experimental Fighting Biplane," it was specially designed so that a machine gun could be mounted in the nose. When war broke out in Europe in August 1914, Vickers were contracted to produce 50 of their FB.5s and by 1915 over 100 had been sent to France with the RFC squadrons, primarily instructed to ram any Zeppelins encountered on their way. Without parachutes, this was not an exciting prospect for the untrained pilots, who resourcefully wore car tires in case they came down in the English Channel. Before long two-seater planes were carrying observers with rifles and revolvers trained on the enemy, and combat aircraft became a reality. All this must have been a great shock to the generals and politicians who had written off airplanes as useless in wartime.

ZEPPELIN AIRSHIPS

Before World War I began in 1914 the idea of airplanes in war was remote, but the use of airships was a possibility. Both the German Army and Navy used airships, and from 1915 they used them to drop bombs on Britain. It took airplanes to shoot them down.

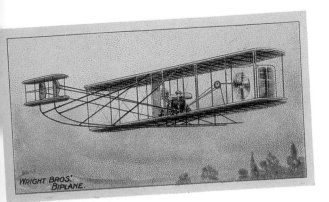

WRIGHT BROS. BIPLANE.

WRIGHT BIPLANE

In August 1910 Lt. Jake Fickel, of the U.S. Army, flew as a passenger in a Wright biplane and fired four shots from a Springfield rifle at a target almost one yard (1m) square on the ground. He scored two hits. He was the first man ever to fire a gun from an airplane.

THE PILOT'S SIDEARM

After the War began most reconnaissance pilots carried a personal "sidearm," for possible use to avoid capture after being shot down. This Webley pistol was a favorite for British pilots.

EXPÉRIENCES DE LANCEMENT DE BOMBES EN AÉROPLANE

THE FRENCH AIR CORPS

This illustration depicts early maneuvers by
the French Air Corps in 1913, showing them
dropping bombs from airplanes.

VICKERS GUNBUS

In February 1913
what could be called
the first British military
aircraft was put on display
by Vickers at an Aero Show in London. This
"Experimental Fighting Biplane" (EFB) had
quite a short central body (a "nacelle") with
the engine at the back driving a pusher
propeller. This meant that the tail had to be
attached by four thin rods (called booms),
which were far enough apart to leave room for
the propeller. This rather strange arrangement
was adopted so that the company's own
Vickers-Maxim machine gun could be mounted
in the nose, fed by a long belt of ammunition.
It was aimed by a gunner in the front cockpit.
Just behind him was the pilot. This "pusher"
arrangement was later used by many types of
aircraft, including the FB.5 (Fighting Biplane,
type 5), popularly called the Gunbus,
which was active in World War I.

GUNBUS COCKPIT

Pilots soon discovered that they needed
instruments to help them fly. The first
were a tachometer (showing how fast the
engine was turning), an altimeter
(showing how high the airplane was
flying), and an airspeed indicator
(showing speed through the air).

Dawn of Air Warfare

DROPPING BOMBS

The first bombers were often ordinary aircraft fitted with a bomb-dropping mechanism invented and fitted on the spot. An even simpler answer was for the crew to hang the bombs beside the cockpits and drop them by hand.

In 1912 the British Government decided that perhaps airplanes might have some military use. They organized a competition, entered by Geoffrey de Havilland with his B.E.1. Although he did not win, he continued to improve his neat biplane which became the Royal Flying Corps' most numerous type in World War I. It was a B.E. that was to claim the first air combat victory on August 25, 1914, only three weeks after the start of the War. Three B.E.2s chased a German aircraft for miles before the German pilot, realizing he could not get away, landed in a field. Both occupants escaped to a nearby wood. The British pilots ran after them, brandishing pistols, but returned to set fire to the enemy aircraft and then took off again. A month later, Frenchman Sergeant Joseph Frantz suddenly came up behind a German Aviatik. His Voisin airplane was armed with a Hotchkiss machine gun. Quickly his observer, Corporal Louis Quénault, aimed at the enemy aircraft and shot it down. This was the first aircraft actually shot down in air warfare, and the dawn of the airplane as a weapon of war.

MACHINE GUN

It was the machine gun that transformed airplanes into fighters. In World War I almost all the machine guns fitted to aircraft were originally designed for use by soldiers on the ground. Many French aircraft used this type of Hotchkiss machine gun, mounted on pivots and aimed by the observer. He was usually in a cockpit behind the pilot, but in the Voisin he was in front.

THE "BLÉRIOT EXPERIMENTAL" OR B.E.2

Blériot was a Frenchman who made monoplanes, but his name became synonymous with the R.F.C. for airplanes with a propeller on the nose. De Havilland's B.E.2 was popular with the R.F.C. It was very stable in flight, which meant it could fly without the pilot touching the controls. Therefore both pilot and observer could watch the battlefield below and write down anything of interest. This stability made the aircraft difficult to maneuver, which was disastrous against the new German planes in World War I.

NATIONAL MARKINGS c.1915

Once the War began it was soon realized that aircraft had to be painted with a clear indication of their nationality, so ground soldiers did not shoot at their own aircraft. Soon simple national markings were devised.

| Great Britain | Russia | Belgium | Italy | Germany |

MONOPLANE FIGHTERS

The British thought monoplanes unsafe, but the French Morane-Saulnier firm made them in large numbers. This Type L monoplane had the wing passing through the fuselage (body), while other Moranes had it fixed above the fuselage on struts.

RECORD BREAKERS

At the end of World War I, there were many unwanted, cheap aircraft available producing a situation that was right for development, adventure, and innovation. Races such as the Schneider Trophy were resumed after the war, and now there were plenty of trained pilots (both men and women) to challenge existing records. Aviators saw opportunities for establishing new records in every corner of the world. The 1920s and 1930s saw new airways opened, and slowly and steadily the world grew smaller. Media interest was at its height, and the excitement generated by these record breakers and pioneers spread worldwide.

THE DARLING OF THE PEOPLE

In 1928, the Australian Bert Hinkler flew from London, England to Darwin, Australia, prompting a young working-class British woman to vow to do the same. Amy Johnson (1903–1941) and her fisherman father scraped together enough money to purchase a Gypsy Moth. Johnson achieved her goal in 1930, and although she took four days longer than Hinkler, she was the first woman to fly the route solo and became the "Darling of the people." Crowds flocked to see her, and songs and poems were written about her.

THE DE HAVILLAND GYPSY MOTH

The de Havilland Gypsy Moth was Great Britain's most popular light aircraft. Amy Johnson named hers "Jason" and painted it dark green, her lucky color. Her Moth was considered much too small for the journey she had in mind, but remarkably the plane made it intact.

ALCOCK AND BROWN

Captain John Alcock and Lieutenant Arthur Whitten-Brown were the first to fly nonstop across the Atlantic Ocean on June 14, 1919. It proved to be an epic journey. They took off from Newfoundland, and almost right away, their problems began. The radio failed; their specially heated suits were not working; and a section of exhaust fell off. When they hit bad weather, Alcock took the plane high to avoid snow clouds. The engines began to get blocked by ice, so Brown had to clamber along the wing and chip away the ice with a knife several times. They were hugely relieved when they finally landed in Ireland (unfortunately, in a bog), 16 hours after takeoff. A statue stands at Heathrow Airport, in England, honoring their achievement.

THE FIRST SOLO ATLANTIC CROSSING

Charles Lindbergh took off from Roosevelt Field in New York on May 20, 1927. He was unprepared for the journey, but when he heard that the weather conditions were going to be good, he seized the opportunity. There to see him take off was Anthony Fokker, who was so convinced that Lindbergh would not make it over the trees, let alone across the Atlantic Ocean, he went to the end of the runway to help with the rescue. But the greatest difficulty Lindbergh faced was staying awake; he had to keep opening the side window and pinching himself. He landed in Paris, France 33.5 hours later. He was the 92nd person to cross the Atlantic Ocean by air, but the first to fly solo. He instantly became famous.

CHARLES LINDBERGH (1902–1974)

Charles Lindbergh was probably the most famous aviator of his time. He began his flying career delivering the mail. When the Orteig prize of $25,000 was announced for the first person to cross the Atlantic Ocean, Lindbergh decided to enter. He had difficulty obtaining a plane as the main manufacturers would not risk a plane on an unknown pilot. With the help of some businessmen, he approached Ryan Aircraft who agreed to modify their single-engine M62 to his specification. In return for their help, the businessmen had one request, that he name the plane after their city. He called it *The Spirit of Saint Louis*. The plane was built in two months at a cost of $6,000.

POLE TO POLE

Polar exploration and aviation were seen as the big adventures of the age. The Norwegian Roald Amundsen was the first man to reach the South Pole on foot and then wanted to conquer the North Pole. He did so in an airship, which had been built by the Italian Umberto Nobile in 1928.

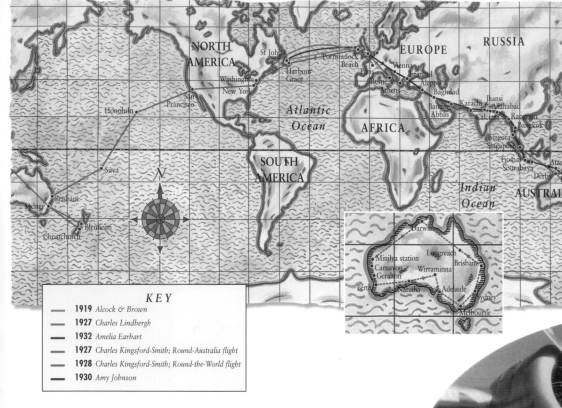

AMELIA EARHART (1898–1937)

American Amelia Earhart was the first woman to cross the Atlantic Ocean in a plane in 1928, albeit as a passenger. It fueled her enthusiasm to become a pilot, and in 1932, she became the first-ever woman to fly the journey solo. She was also the first to fly solo from Hawaii to San Francisco in 1935, when many pilots had tried and failed. In March 1937, Amelia set off with a crew to circumnavigate the globe in a Lockheed *Electra (right)*. All went well until they took off from Papua New Guinea, and the plane simply disappeared!

THE SOUTHERN CROSS

In 1927, two Australian wartime pilots made a record-breaking flight round Australia. Charles Kingsford-Smith and Charles Ulm completed the journey, which covered 7,457 mi. (12,000km), in just over ten days. They quickly announced their next record attempt—to fly across the Pacific Ocean. In their Fokker trimotor airplane called the Southern Cross, the two men took off from San Francisco on May 31, 1928 with two American crewmembers. Making stops on the Pacific islands of Honolulu and Suva, they finally landed in Brisbane, Australia on June 9. They went on to complete the round-the-world trip.

RECORD BREAKERS

The race for the pioneers was not only to reach new countries. By the 1930s, they were also competing to fly the farthest, the fastest, the highest, and to stay in the air the longest. In 1932, Professor Auguste Piccard took his hot-air balloon to a height of 56,000 ft. (17,000m) but, as with other records, it was soon broken. The following year a Russian high-altitude balloon reached 62,300 ft. (19,000m). Wiley Post and Harold Getty set a record in 1931 for circling the globe in a Lockheed *Vega* in just eight and half days. McCready and Kelly established an endurance record by staying aloft in their Fokker monoplane for 38 hours. And the speed records were being continually smashed at the many air races.

FLYING HIGH

Auguste Piccard, seen here celebrating his 49th birthday with a topical cake, held the high-altitude record in 1932. This was a great achievement, as there were no modern safeguards on board his balloon. There was a huge risk of physical injury as his capsule was not pressurized, as modern aircraft are today. The higher one flies, the lower the air density and pressure, and so he was risking burst blood vessels, burst eardrums, and even blackouts.

"WRONG WAY" CORRIGAN

Douglas Corrigan was a mechanic who had once shaken hands with Lindbergh and ever since had been determined to follow in his footsteps, or rather his air route. The problem was he had neither a plane nor the means to obtain one. He bought a Curtiss Robin for $300 and worked at repairing and improving it. He attached most of the electronic instruments on to the panel with tape and wire, and attached fuel tanks on the front of his plane, which meant that he couldn't clearly see where he was going. When he applied for a license to cross the Atlantic Ocean, unsurprisingly he was refused. He wished the inspector a "bon voyage" and flew off, claiming he was returning home. An hour later he was spotted crossing the Atlantic Ocean. He landed in Ireland the next day, saying that his compass had malfunctioned and so he'd gone the wrong way. "Wrong Way" Corrigan, as he became known, received a ticker-tape reception when he returned home to New York and was made an honorary member of the Liars' Club.

DEWOITINE D.520

In 1939 the French Dewoitine
company began making the D.520,
generally considered the best
French fighter of World War II.
Its 910-horsepower engine was
made by Hispano-Suiza, and it
was specially arranged so that a
big 0.8in (20mm) cannon could fit
on top of the crankcase firing
through the hub of the propeller.
The D.520 also had two machine
guns in each wing, and had a top speed
of 329 mph (530 km/h).

BOEING F4B-1

The F4B family were U.S. Navy counterparts
of the Hawker Fury. They had another kind of engine in which
the cylinders were arranged radially like the spokes of a wheel
and covered in thin fins so that they could be cooled by air. The resulting aircraft looked much less streamlined,
but in fact the air-cooled radial was usually lighter. As it was also shorter it made the fighter more
maneuverable, and it did not need a heavy drag-producing water radiator.

THE CHANGING ENGINE

In World War I many fighters had rotary engines
such as the 130-horsepower Clerget (left). The
entire engine rotated together with the propeller,
and this acted like a top (a gyroscope) and made
piloting difficult. After 1918 designers made
static radials, such as the 450-horsepower Bristol
Jupiter (right). Apart from having nine instead
of seven cylinders, this differed in using
ordinary gasoline without lubricating
oil having to be added.

BETWEEN THE WORLD WARS

World War I ended on November 11, 1918. For the next ten years there was little pressure to build better fighters, though engines developed dramatically. This development was further spurred by air racing. In 1931 a 2,780 horsepower engine was developed for racing by Rolls Royce. It could only maintain this power for minutes at a time however, and required special fuels. Compared to the 130-horsepower engines on some fighters in World War I, this was a huge leap and triggered the development of much better fuels for air force squadrons. Also, by 1930, a few designers were finding out how to make aircraft with a metal skin. The wire-braced biplanes of the past had fabric covering and these were replaced by all-metal "stressed-skin" monoplanes. This so dramatically reduced drag that fighter speeds jumped from 200 mph (322 km/h) to over 350 mph (563 km/h). In turn this led to cockpits covered by transparent canopies, improved engine installations, flaps on the wings to slow the landing, and landing gears that could retract in flight. Some of these developments were opposed by fighter pilots, who could not believe that a fighter could be a sleek monoplane with an enclosed cockpit.

POLIKARPOV I-153

This Soviet biplane was unusual among biplanes in having retractable landing gear. The wheels folded directly backwards, at the same time rotating through 90 degrees so that they could lie flat in the underside of the aircraft. The I-153 had a radial engine, but it was enclosed in a neat cowling to reduce drag. Thus, this fighter could reach 267 mph (430 km/h), about 62 mph (100 km/h) faster than the Fury and F4B.

HAWKER FURIES

In the days before jet aircraft there were two basic kinds of engine. Some had their cylinders (usually 12) cooled by water and arranged in two lines. When installed in the aircraft they resulted in a long and pointed nose, as in these Fury fighters of the Royal Air Force (R.A.F.) in 1932. This looked very streamlined, but in fact to cool the water such engines needed a big radiator and this slowed the aircraft down.

COMMERCIAL FLIGHT

Once the pioneers had opened up the air routes, commercial aviation developed swiftly. Carrying mail was one of the first commercial uses for aircraft, and it wasn't long before passenger flights were on the increase. In 1937, Imperial Airways started the first commercial air service across the Atlantic Ocean with two Short "C"-Class flying boats. Flying boats were used when destinations were near suitable stretches of water, thus saving the cost of building expensive airfields. The pioneers of commercial flight were not only the pilots, they included the designers, engineers, and those who understood the science of flight.

PAN AMERICAN AIRWAYS

Pan American World Airways was started by businessman Juan Trippe in 1922. He was not especially interested in aviation, but like others around the world, he recognized the future role of the airplane. Trippe was constantly looking to improve his planes and his service. Pan Am was one of the first operators to order a jetliner in 1953—the Boeing 707–120.

THE DC2/3

In the stick-and-string days of the past, airplanes were often designed and built in a few weeks. If they didn't work, they were pulled to pieces, redesigned, and rebuilt. But the new airlines demanded bigger and better aircraft to suit the needs of the increasing number of travelers. Manufacturing firms, like Douglas and Boeing, began to build passenger craft, and the Douglas DC2/3 became the leading airliner for the next 20 years.

AIRSHIP TRAVEL

The 1920s and 1930s were golden eras for airships, the two most famous being the Graf Zeppelin and the Hindenburg. They carried thousands of passengers across the Atlantic Ocean for several years. Then, in 1937, the Hindenburg set off from Berlin, Germany en route to the U.S.A. As it came in to land, there was an explosion and the entire ship quickly went up in flames. Incredibly, 61 of the 97 passengers survived, but people lost confidence, bringing the airship era to an abrupt end.

2 TAGEN NACH NORD-AMERIKA!
DEUTSCHE ZEPPELIN-REEDEREI

THE AIRDROME

The aircraft was not always first choice for travel in the 1930s. One of the problems was the placing of airfields. It often took longer to get to and from the airdrome than the flight itself, and other forms of transportation, like the train, ship, and car, were also developing. Berlin Airport, shown here in 1937, was one of the first to be purpose built. Croydon Airport was one of the biggest, and by 1939, Imperial Airways was offering services to far-away destinations such as Karachi, Cape Town, Lake Victoria, Singapore, and Brisbane.

THE MAIL MAN

The first mail flights were between New York and Chicago in surplus warplanes bought by the U.S. Post Office. In the first year, 18 pilots were killed and fears grew that the service would be closed down. In 1921, to demonstrate its value, a cross-country flight from San Francisco to New York was organized, with a pilot named Jack Knight due to take over one of the planes in Nebraska. Bonfires were lit to guide the flight and a relief pilot was arranged, but the flight was so delayed that the bonfires had fizzled out, and his relief pilot had gone home. Knight took two mouthfuls of coffee and, with only some road maps to guide him, flew on in the dark, reaching Chicago at 8 a.m. The mail was transferred and reached New York in a record time of 33 hours and 20 minutes. It would have taken 72 hours by train. The airmail service was secured.

COMFORT IN THE AIR

The Boeing Airplane Company was started by William Boeing in 1917. In 1933, the Boeing 247 became the first modern commercial airplane. It was all metal, low winged, and had twin engines. It was also the first airliner with retractable landing gear. With its soundproof, heated cabin, and upholstered seats, its ten passengers traveled in comfort that had never been previously experienced.

THE AIRLINES OF EUROPE

Many countries were developing airlines in the 1930s. Various European airlines set about extending their routes to their colonies, offering scheduled services around the world.

AVIA
HOLLANDSCHE GENEVER
SCHIEDAM
REGISTERED

SCRAMBLE!

These two Canadian pilots are scrambling for takeoff in their Hurricanes during the Battle of Britain. Grabbing their helmets and parachutes, they were in the air within minutes. The Royal Canadian Air Force fought with the British Royal Air Force throughout the war. Canada participated in the Commonwealth Air Training Plan, which trained 132,000 members of air crew.

THE MESSERSCHMITT BF 109 B

The Messerschmitt BF 109 played a significant part in the war. It was designed by Willy Messerschmitt, a young pilot who had learned his skills as a glider pilot. He was able to develop his talents with the encouragement of the German Air Ministry. The Messerschmitt first flew in 1937 and was active against the Allies in the Battle of Britain. It is estimated that 35,000 Messerschmitt BF 109s were built. A few can be seen in museums today.

BATTLE OF BRITAIN

The Battle of Britain is considered to be one of the greatest historic battles. For almost two months, 740 British and Allied pilots fought 3,500 German Luftwaffe pilots over the skies of Great Britain. Most of the Messerschmitts 109s fuel was used up reaching Great Britain and so were not able to continue the fight for as long as the Allied pilots. Having lost the battle, the German superiority in the air had been destroyed. The chance of a quick victory over Great Britain had gone forever, as well as the fear of invasion faded.

ENOLA GAY

Most American aircrew named the airplanes in which they flew. The *Enola Gay* was the name given to the Boeing B29 Superfortress piloted by Colonel Paul Tibbets. It dropped the first atom bomb on Hiroshima, destroying the city and killing 100,000 people. Three days later, another atom bomb was dropped in Nagasaki, forcing the Japanese to surrender on August 14, 1945.

PEARL HARBOR

Although the two countries were not at war, Japanese dive-bombers, operating from six aircraft carriers, attacked and destroyed the American Pacific Fleet at anchor in Pearl Harbor on December 7, 1941. This brought the U.S.A. into the war. Aircraft carriers were not unknown in World War I, but by World War II, they were a major part of air and sea warfare.

WORLD WAR II

World War II saw rapid developments in aviation technology. Communication, navigation, radio, and radar were all developed and improved during the war years, as was the design of the aircraft and the engines. German bombing raids in World War I had shown that the airplane could be used as an instrument of total war. The Italians used bombing tactics against ground soldiers in Abyssinia (Ethiopia) in 1936. And in the Spanish Civil War of 1937–1939 the most advanced fighter plane of the time—the German Messerschmitt BF 109—made its debut, and was to have a significant effect in World War II. It was the first airplane to be used as an offensive weapon. The first British fighters to confront the German Messerschmitts were the Hurricanes and Spitfires, and the scene was set for the greatest air battle ever fought—the Battle of Britain. World War II firmly established the use of aircraft in warfare.

SPITFIRE

One of the most famous fighters ever built was the Spitfire. It was designed by R.J. Mitchell, who had earned his reputation designing the record-breaking British Schneider seaplanes. Outnumbered by the Hurricane in the Battle of Britain, its superior performance was directed at the escorting Messerschmitts, allowing the Hurricanes to attack the German bombers.

NEVER HAS SO MUCH BEEN OWED BY SO MANY TO SO FEW

Winston Churchill recognized the importance of all the Allied pilots who fought in the Battle of Britain. The Germans underestimated the determined spirit of the Spitfire and Hurricane pilots. Flying aces emerged, but the British Royal Air Force was reluctant to name them—all who flew were heroes. They were the first pilots to successfully fly modern planes in combat to safeguard their country.

31

THE FIRST JETS

Toward the end of World War II, the engines of the latest war planes were cumbersome masses of metal weighing over a ton, yet with every part made like a fine Swiss watch. Even though the latest fighters had become heavier, the massive engines could propel them at over 450 mph (724 km/h).

The difficulty was that it was almost impossible to make traditional fighters go any faster. Even more serious was the fact that ordinary propellers were reaching a fundamental speed limit. Thus the fighters of 1944–1945 were the end of an era. In both Great Britain and Germany the turbojet engine was being developed. Frank Whittle had invented the first turbojet engine in Great Britain in 1929 but nobody was interested. Six years later in Germany, Hans von Ohain thought of the same idea, and the first jet aircraft flew in Germany in August 1939. Nothing much happened to Whittle's engine until one was sent to the USA. Then things moved fast, and the first Allied jet fighter, the American Bell P-59 Airacomet, flew on October 2, 1942. However, the much greater German effort resulted in a shoal of jet aircraft. The most important was the Messerschmitt Me 262, and had the Germans not been defeated in 1945 their jets would have been a big problem for the Allies.

A NEW BREED OF PILOT

R.P. "Bee" Beamont was a fighter pilot throughout the War, and afterward he became even more famous in Britain as a test pilot. He tested Hawker Typhoons and Tempests, followed by Gloster Meteor jets, and many other types, before becoming Chief Test Pilot on the Canberra jet bomber, Lightning, TSR.2, Jaguar, and Tornado.

LAVOCHKIN LA-7

At the end of World War II the Russians had no jet aircraft, and typical of their fighters was the La-7, powered by a 2,000-horsepower piston engine. For the desperately harsh conditions on the Russian front aircraft had to be very tough and simple. The La-7 was nevertheless at least equal to fighters from any other country.

ROCKET INTERCEPTOR

The Messerschmitt Me 163B was a strange tailless rocket interceptor with the pilot in the nose along with two 0.9in (30mm) cannon. Behind him were tons of deadly liquids which fed a rocket engine in the tail. It was a tricky "last-ditch" weapon which killed many of its own pilots.

FE500

GLOSTER METEOR

First of the British jets, the Gloster Meteor
had two Whittle-type engines, and first flew
in March 1943. This was one of the
prototypes, as indicated by the big
"P" in a circle. After the War a later
version set a speed record at
over 616 mph (975 km/h).

MESSERSCHMITT
ME 262A-1A

The Me 262 was a superb all-round fighter and
fighter-bomber powered by two Jumo 004B turbojets
slung under the wings. In the nose was the formidable
armament of four 30mm cannon. With a speed of 525
mph (845 km/h), it was much faster than any Allied
aircraft. The Me 262 would have been even more of
a problem to the Allies had not Adolf Hitler misguidedly
decreed that they all be used as bombers.

SIR FRANK WHITTLE

As a young and very junior RAF pilot in 1929
Frank Whittle invented the turbojet. He proved
mathematically that it could work, but his
superiors in the Air Ministry were not
interested. At his own expense he took out a
patent, finally granted in January 1930, but
still nobody showed the slightest interest. At
last, in desperation, he and a group of
friends found just enough money actually to
build a turbojet, which he started up on
April 12, 1937. This amazed the officials
and experts, but by this time hundreds of
engineers were working on jets in Germany,
and theirs was the first jet aircraft to fly.

THE AIRPLANE COMES OF AGE

World War II saw an acceleration in the innovation and development of aircraft. In six years, guided missiles and nuclear weapons had supplemented machine guns and high-explosive bombs; the piston engine was replaced by the gas turbine (turbojets). The principle of the jet engine had been known for some time, and by the end of World War II, it was being used on military planes by both sides. Plans were also being considered for the first commercial passenger jets. Speed became a new challenge. In 1924, the speed record was 278 mph (447km/h). By 1934 the speed record was 440 mph (707km/h). Charles (Chuck) Yeager broke the sound barrier in the Bell X-1, which was called *Glamorous Glennis* after his wife.

ENGINES TODAY

The Whittle turbojet became the forerunner of today's fast, modern engines.

BREAKING THE SOUND BARRIER

Chuck Yeager, an American war veteran, was an outstanding test pilot of his time. On October 14, 1947, the Bell X-1 was lifted into the air by a mother plane—a B29—to conserve fuel. On being released, Yeager opened up the four-chamber rocket engines for an all-out attempt to reach supersonic flight.

DE HAVILLAND'S COMET

De Havilland had always been an innovative company and, in 1949, the first pure jetliner, *Comet 1*, left Heathrow Airport, England. In 1952, it began its first scheduled flights but was temporarily withdrawn from service two years later following a series of crashes. The cause was traced to fuselage fatigue problems, which were overcome, and some are still flying for the military today.

REFUELING IN MIDAIR

Endurance and distance records, as well as transatlantic flights, prompted the technology of aerial refueling. The Harrow Tanker provided the first service in 1939, and now it is common practice for jet fighters to refuel in midair.

THE JUMBO JET

In 1952, the first jet-liner had 44 seats. By the 1970s, wide-body jets were revolutionizing commercial air travel. The Boeing 747 was at the forefront of these new jet aircraft. With 350 seats or more, they were given the name jumbo jets. Today, the largest jumbo jet is the Airbus A380.

FRANK WHITTLE
(1907–1996)

Like two other young engineers in Germany, Pabst von Obain and Werner von Braun, Frank Whittle knew that the principle of a jet engine was similar to rocket propulsion. Whilst two Germans were developing their own ideas, Whittle was struggling to gain any encouragement from the British Air Ministry. In 1937, the first successful test run of his jet engine took place and the Air Ministry started to take an interest. But it was the Germans who developed the first jet aircraft in 1939, with the Heinkel HE 178. Two years later, Whittle's engine was tested on the Gloster E28/39.

SUPERSONIC FLIGHT

There are many problems with supersonic flight. Air becomes so compressed that it forms solid shock waves. Shock waves occur when air flowing over any part of the aircraft reaches supersonic speed—760 mph (1,226km/h) at sea level, decreasing at heights to 660 mph (1,061km/h)—or, more simply, Mach 1. There had been a number of attempts to break the sound barrier without success. Yeager had full confidence in his aircraft and when the needle on his Machmeter swung past Mach 0.94 on to 0.96 to 0.98, he felt the bucking and shuddering of the shock waves, then they suddenly stopped. He had reached Mach 1.05, and the calmer conditions that lie beyond the sound barrier. He described it as an "eerie quiet."

WHITTLE ENGINE

In 1930, Sir Frank Whittle filed his first patent for a jet engine, and on April 12, 1937, his first turbojet had its maiden run. Following many experiments, Whittle could control and test the engine at speeds two or three times faster than a conventional piston engine.

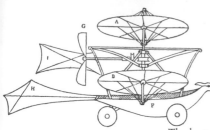

Vertical Lift

The best-known Vertical Take Off and Landing (VTOL) aircraft is the helicopter. The principle of rotary movement lifting a weight upward was well known. Both Leonardo da Vinci and Sir George Cayley had designed helicopters, but it was not until 400 years later that the first one was ever flown. After World War II, Igor Sikorsky designed a single-rotor helicopter and pioneered helicopter trials in Russia. Helicopters have proved invaluable both for the military and the rescue services. Their advantage is that they can hover, take off, rise vertically, and land in a restricted space.

CAYLEY'S DESIGNS

The principle of rotary movement lifting a weight upward was well known. In 1843, Sir George Cayley designed this early helicopter (*above*), but it was never built.

THE NATURAL ROTOR

The idea of rotor power can be seen in nature, as this sycamore seedpod demonstrates. This natural rotor may have provided the inspiration for early helicopter designs.

IGOR SIKORSKY (1889–1972)

Russian-born aviator Igor Sikorsky was the first man to solve the difficulties of "torque"—the reason why earlier helicopter designs had been unsuccessful. The problem was that a machine rotating in one direction will produce a torque reaction in the other direction, so as the rotor blades of a helicopter turned in one direction, the helicopter itself turned in the other. Sikorsky controlled this torque reaction by attaching a small rotor on the tail. He produced the first successful practical helicopter the VS 300 in 1941 in America, when he hovered in the air for 102 minutes. Sikorsky helicopters are used today, based on his original revolutionary design.

HARRIER JUMP JET

The Hawker Siddeley Harrier is a VTOL (Vertical Take Off and Landing) aircraft. Representing significant advances in aircraft design, jet nozzles direct the exhaust downward when taking off and landing.

THE FIRST FLIGHT

In 1907, Paul Cornu, a mechanic from France, became the first person to fly in a helicopter, hovering just off the ground for 20 seconds. However, the fuselage rotated in the opposite direction to the rotor blades, causing him to crash to the ground. His delicate machine broke into many pieces.

THE FLYING BEDSTEAD

The first free-flight demonstration of direct jet lift was given by Rolls Royce in 1954. Their "Flying Bedstead" successfully demonstrated maneuverability in free flight and provided invaluable information and research for the design of the first jump jet.

TO THE RESCUE

Even in the early days, the advantages of helicopters were recognized. Because helicopters can take off and land in a restricted space, and can hover in one place, they have become invaluable in everyday life. Landing on rooftops in busy cities is beneficial to business, but probably their most important role is as a rescue vehicle. They are used by the emergency services for air-sea rescues, mountain rescues, and as air ambulances.

TODAY'S SKIES

Thanks to the pioneers of the past, there isn't a country today that cannot be reached by a jet airliner within 24 hours. Today's airports have to cope with the millions of passengers and aircraft that pass through them each year. Thousands of airplanes can take off from major airports in a day. A huge team of people are on hand to make sure that the planes land safely, are quickly turned around, and sent off on their way again. Today, air travel is a popular and reasonably cheap form of transportation. Airliners are larger and more comfortable. Smaller jets (like the one pictured), are sold to private clients. The skies are controlled with sophisticated systems and international networking to make air travel safer than ever before.

FREQUENT FLIERS

It has taken just over a century, since the first ever controlled flight in 1903, for air travel to become part of everyday life. Most people rarely look up when a plane flies overhead, and many of us think nothing of boarding a plane. At busy airports, planes take off and land every few minutes.

IT'S A SMALL WORLD

Looking back over the last century, we can see it not only as a time when people conquered the air, but a time when the pioneers led us toward an understanding of the world. Air travel really has made the world a smaller place. People from all walks of life are prepared to fly, venturing farther afield and going to remote places that a century before were just names on a map.

CONCORDE

Rather than countries competing against each other as they did in the original race for the skies, many countries are working together, sharing ideas, research, and costs. Concorde, one of the most striking planes of all time, was a joint achievement between France and Great Britain. A technological triumph, Concorde could cruise at twice the speed of sound, flying from London to New York in just 3.5 hours. As a result of cost, pollution, and a single crash, Concorde was retired from service in 2003.

AIR TRAFFIC CONTROL

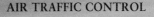

Early aviators relied on Morse code for communication. Radio now provides reliable round-the-world networking, so that pilots can remain constantly in touch with the air traffic controllers. With radar and radio, air travel is one of the safest forms of travel that exists today.

RADAR (RADIO DIRECTION AND RANGE)

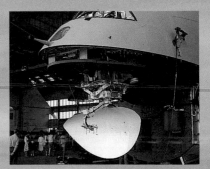

British research had shown that radio waves are reflected by metal objects as early as 1934. It was also discovered that strong, frequent waves could be detected by a suitable receiver. The first radars were large ground stations. Radar proved its worth during the Battle of Britain, as German pilots could not understand how the British knew their movements in advance. By 1941, radar was small enough to fit inside an aircraft and is now so sophisticated, that it is involved with traffic control, collision avoidance, weather warnings, and landing control.

THE PIONEERING SPIRIT

The pioneering spirit still exists today. There are the adventurers who have set out to copy the record-breaking attempts of their predecessors. Louis Blériot, a Parisian solicitor, rebuilt one of his grandfather's aircraft, and in 1998, he attempted to repeat the historical journey of 1909. There are new designs and, new challenges, all of which contribute to keeping the spirit of adventure alive.

STEALTH BOMBER

Military airplanes have developed in speed and performance due to the development of the jet engine. The American Lockheed F-117A Stealth Fighter is designed to be undetectable by enemy radar. Its surfaces are faceted, which enables it to deflect radar signals.

AROUND THE WORLD IN A BALLOON

When Auguste Piccard made his record-breaking, high-altitude flight in his balloon in 1932, he reached a height of 56,000 ft. (17,000m). In 1999, the first round-the-world hot-air balloon ride was recorded. In 2002, Steve Fossett became the first solo balloonist.

FROM MYTH TO REALITY

In 1985, a team of engineers from the Massachusetts Institute of Technology set out to follow the mythical flight of Daedalus in the Greek story of Daedalus and Icarus. Their aim was to fly the 74 mi. (119km) between the Greek islands of Crete and Santorini in a man-powered machine. Their machine was an aircraft with a wingspan as wide as a Boeing 727, but it weighed only 70 lbs (32kg). It was named *Daedalus* and powered by Kanellos Kanellopoulos, a Greek bicycle champion—who was chosen for his amazing endurance. In April 1998, Kanellopoulos pedaled the distance in four hours, splashing down safely just short of land—and set a new world record for human-powered flight.

HOTOL

The British HOTOL (Horizontal Take Off and Landing) vehicle was intended as a rocket-mounted vehicle, able to travel at Mach 7. However, the project was eventually withdrawn. The Reaction Engines Skylon is the newest project.

VOYAGER

In 1986, a new long-distance aviation record was set when Dick Rutan and Jeana Yeager flew nonstop around the world without refueling. This took them just nine days in their aircraft, Voyager. When they landed, they had just 37 gallons of fuel left in the tanks, which had contained 1,200 gallons on takeoff.

FLIGHT OF THE FUTURE?

A passenger plane that flies at hypersonic speed on the edges of space may appear in the near future. NASA had been investigating the National Aerospace Plane (right), which could fly at 6,500 mph (10,461 km/h)—ten times the speed of sound. However, this project was canceled due to safety concerns and budget costs.

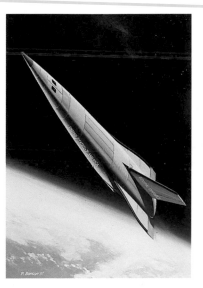

PIONEERS OF THE AIR -A TIMELINE-

~1939~

First transatlantic mail service begins

The Heinkel HE178 becomes the first jet-powered aircraft

~1940~

Battle of Britain takes place

~1941~

Igor Sikorsky designs a single-rotor helicopter

Gloster E28/39 is tested

~1945~

Atomic bomb is dropped on Hiroshima

~1947~

Chuck Yeager breaks sound barrier

~1949~

The first jet-engine liner, Comet 1, is unveiled

~1954~

Rolls Royce demonstrates the first direct jet lift with their Flying Bedstead

~1986~

Dick Rutan and Jeana Yeager fly nonstop around world without refueling

~1998~

The Daedalus project sets the record for the longest man-powered flight.

DID YOU KNOW?

Marco Polo started his journey from China to Portugal in 1275. It took five years. Today, that same journey by airplane takes five hours.

The Wright Brothers named their plane the Flyer after the most successful bicycle that they had built in their workshops.

W. W. Balantyne is reputed to have been the first aerial stowaway. He was a crew member of the R34 airship, but was taken off at the last minute to lighten the load. Determined to be on the ship as it attempted to cross the Atlantic, he hid in the rigging between two gas bags. Unfortunately, breathing in the hydrogen made him sick and he had to give himself up. He was then made to work his passage for the rest of the journey.

In 1930 the F.A. Cup Final between Arsenal and Huddersfield had to be stopped for 20 minutes while the *Graf Zeppelin* flew overhead.

Alan Cobham set off to fly to Australia from Great Britain in 1926. A sandstorm forced him to fly low over Iraq and Bedouin tribesman, who had never seen an airplane before, tried to shoot it down. Unfortunately a bullet hit the co-pilot who later died in hospital.

A second stowaway, the ship's cat called Wopsie, was also found. They were both feted when the airship finally landed in the U.S.A.

Galbraith Rodgers set off to fly from New York to California in a Baby Wright plane in 1911. The journey took 50 days and he made 69 stops, 16 of which were crash landings. Wherever he stopped, people rushed to take souvenirs from the plane, so it was

The Flying Fraulein was a young German woman called Hanna Reisch who received an Iron Cross from Hitler. Her first love was gliding and she could manage the gliders as well as, if not better, than her male counterparts. She became a test pilot on both planes and helicopters, and became the first woman in Germany to be given airforce rank.

The Anatov, An225 is the heaviest aircraft ever to fly. It has a 130 foot (40 metre) long cargo-hold and each of its six engines delivers a 54,000 lb (24,494 kg) thrust.

fortunate that the ground crew had plenty of spare parts. When he finally reached California, only two pieces of the original plane were left.

In the Soviet Union bombers were fitted with fighters to protect them. Vladimir Vakhmistrov conducted experiments that in November 1935 culminated in a TB-3 heavy bomber taking off with an I-15 biplane fighter on top of each wing and an I-16 monoplane fighter under each wing. An I-Z monoplane fighter then approached and hooked on under the fuselage, to make five fighters joined to one bomber! If enemy aircraft appeared they were all to unlatch and zoom off.

Arguments have raged over which was the first jet fighter. The first to fly was the German Heinkel He 280, which never went into production. The first to be delivered to a customer was the American Bell YP-59A Airacomet, delivered to the United States Army Air Force (U.S.A.A.F.) on September 30, 1943. The first delivered to a front-line regular squadron was the British Gloster Meteor, to 616 Squadron on July 12, 1944. And yet most

experts think it should be the German Me 262. Suffice to say, in the Second World War, the Me 262 was the best jet fighter, and by far the most numerous. The XF-85 Goblin unfolded its wings in flight. This tiny jet fighter had folding wings to fit inside one of the B-36 bomb bays. If enemy fighters appeared, the XF-85 was to be released. After dropping like a stone, its pilot would unfold the wings and do battle with the enemy. Afterwards he was to hook back on for the long ride home.

The fastest fighter in regular service was the Soviet Union's MiG-25. Powered by two huge R-15B-300 engines, it could fly long distances at 1,864 mph (3,000 km/h), or nearly three times the speed of sound.

In 1914 Pemberton-Billing designed, built and test-flew a successful fighter in seven days. The corresponding time for the development of the Eurofighter is 20 years (1982–2002).

In both World Wars a typical effective life for a fighter was two months. Today the RAF Jaguars are to serve 40 years (1972–2012), while the German Bachem Ba349 of 1944 was designed to fly a single mission only.

GLOSSARY

Above Ground Level (AGL) Distance of the aircraft above the ground.

Above Sea Level (ASL) Distance of the aircraft above mean sea level.

accuracy A measure of exactness, possibly expressed in percentages.

air pressure The force of air on things.

air traffic controllers People who monitor and control air traffic within a particular area.

aircraft A craft that flies in the air; either fixed or rotary wing.

aircraft carrier A large ship with a flat deck on which airplanes can take off and land.

airship An aircraft that is lighter than air and can be steered. An airship has an engine and is filled with gas.

altimeter A device to measure altitude.

altitude The height of a thing above earth or above sea level.

ammunition The objects fired from any weapon, or material that can be exploded. Bullets, bombs, and gunpowder are types of ammunition.

armament The total military power of a country, including weapons and supplies.

attitude The primary aircraft angles in the state vector; pitch, roll, and yaw.

autopilot A mode of an automatic flight control system which controls primary flight controls to meet specific mission objectives.

aviation The act, practice, or science of flying airplanes.

aviator A person who flies an aircraft; a pilot.

barometric altitude Height with respect to fixed earth reference (above mean sea level).

barometric pressure Height with respect to fixed earth reference (barometric altitude, feet above mean sea level).

beacon A device, usually based on the ground, that aids in determining position or direction.

bearing Direction on a compass. The course that an aircraft adopts.

biplane An airplane with two pairs of wings, one above the other.

body The aircraft, usually referring to a coordinate system.

body coordinates Coordinates referenced to the body of the aircraft.

Calibrated Airspeed (CAS) Indicated airspeed which is corrected for instrumentation errors.

cockpit The area from which the pilot and crew control an airplane.

Data Transfer System (DTS) A device for transferring data with avionics, similar to a diskette drive.

dead reckoning (DR) A method of navigation based on basic information (barometric altitude, magnetic heading, airspeed, wind conditions) from the best available sources; sometimes short for air data dead reckoning.

discrete time Time divided into quantized intervals; in avionics, time is usually divided into equal intervals to create a periodic process.

drag The force caused by air on a moving object (air resistance).

earth coordinates Coordinates referenced to the earth.

earth data Environmental data related to the earth at some point of interest; usually a function of latitude and longitude.

earth radius The radius of the earth, a function of position; separate radii for longitudinal radius and for lateral radius.

earthspeed Total velocity measured with respect to a plane tangent to the earth's surface at the current position.

elevation An angle in the vertical plane through a longitudinal axis; height above mean sea level, usually of terrain.

FCS Flight control system.

fixed wing An airplane, as opposed to a rotary wing/ helicopter.

flaps A control surface on fixed-wing aircraft, usually mounted to the fore edge of the wings, that extends the wing to provide added lift at low speeds.

Flight Control System (FCS) A primary flight control system or an automatic flight control system.

flight controls Controls in a cockpit for flying an aircraft.

fly over A position update by flying directly over a known point.

fuselage The body of an airplane.

glider A light aircraft without a motor that flies on air currents.

Global Positioning System (GPS) A navigation sensor based on satellites.

groundspeed The speed over the ground; earthspeed projected to a horizontal plane.

gyroscope (gyro) An inertial device for measuring change of attitude (pitch rate, roll rate, and yaw rate).

heading Direction on a compass that an aircraft is pointed.

instrumentation Hardware to measure and to monitor a system.

latitude Position on earth, north or south of the equator.

leg A segment of a flight plan; flight path between two waypoints.

longitude Position on earth, east or west of the prime meridian.

Mach number Ratio of airspeed to the local speed of sound (Mach 1 is the speed of sound under current atmospheric conditions).

magnetic heading Heading of the aircraft relative to magnetic north.

monoplane An airplane with one pair of wings.

Morse code A code in which letters are represented by combinations of long and short signals of light or sound.

nacelle An enclosure on an aircraft.

orientation Direction in reference to a coordinate.

patent A government grant that gives someone the right to make, use, or sell an invention. A patent is given for a certain number of years.

pioneer A person that is the first to do something.

piston engine A part of an engine that moves up and down within a tight sleeve in order to make the machine work.

pressure Barometric air pressure.

prototype A first model of something.

propeller A device used to make an airplane move forward. It is made of tilted blades that are attached to and spin around a hub.

radar The use of radio waves to track the location, distance, and speed of far-away objects. Waves are sent out and then picked up again when they bounce back after hitting some object.

reconnaissance The military observation of a region to locate an enemy.

rotary Having a part or parts that turn on an axis.

rendezvous To meet with another aircraft in the air, for refueling or other mission objectives.

supersonic Indicates a speed which is greater than the speed of sound.

tachometer A device for measuring angular velocity.

take off The action of becoming airborne.

throttle A flight control operated by moving fore or aft with hands, primarily to control thrust (speed) in fixed-wing aircraft.

triplane An airplane with three pairs of wings, one above the other.

waypoint A point on the ground, predefined as a point of interest for the flight; a basic guidance mode, providing lateral guidance to a waypoint.

FURTHER READING & WEBSITES

BOOKS

Air Pioneers (History Makers)
Neil Morris (Chrysalis Education, 2003)

Air Warfare (Modern Warfare)
Martin J. Dougherty (Gareth Stevens Publishing, 2010)

Amelia Earhart: A Life in Flight (Sterling Biographies)
Victoria Garrett Jones (Sterling, 2009)

Amelia Earhart: True Lives
Andrew Langley (Oxford University Press, U.S., 2009)

*Amelia Earhart, Young Air Pioneer
(Young Patriots series)*
Jane Moore Howe and Cathy Morrison (Patria Press, Inc., 2000)

Book of Flight: The Smithsonian National Air and Space Museum Judith E. Rinard (Firefly Books, 2007)

Daredevils of the Air: Thrilling Tales of Pioneer Aviators (Avisson Young Adult Series)
Karen E. Bledsoe (Avisson Press Inc., 2003)

Feathers, Flaps, and Flops: Fabulous Early Fliers
Bo Zaunders and Roxie Munro (Dutton Juvenile, 2001)

*Flight: the Trials and Triumphs of Air Pioneers
(Mega Bites)*
R. G. Grant (Dorling Kindersley Publishers Ltd., 2003)

Flying Machine (DK Eyewitness Books)
Andrew Nahum (DK Children, 2004)

Military Aircraft of WWI (The Story of Flight)
Ole Steen Hansen (Crabtree Publishing Company, 2003)

*Mysterious Journey: Amelia Earhart's Last Flight
(Odyssey: Smithsonian Institution)*
Martha Wickham (Soundprint, 2010)

Seaplanes and Naval Aviation (The Story of Flight)
Ole Steen Hansen (Crabtree Publishing Company, 2003)

Sky Pioneer: A Photobiography of Amelia Earhart
Corinne Szabo (National Geographic Children's Books, 2007)

WEBSITES

www.ueet.nasa.gov/StudentSite/historyofflight.html
Contains information on the history of flight.

www.centennialofflight.gov/user/kids.htm
Explore how our world has changed as a result of the Wright Brothers' first powered flight on December 17, 1903.

www.nasm.si.edu/exhibitions/gal102/americabyair/
National Air and Space Museum—(Smithsonian Institution)
This site has different activities, including a virtual flight across America during different parts of the twentieth century. Visitors can click on the "Fly Across America" to view period documents that depict what the in-flight experience was like from the 1920s to the present. The "Explore Exhibition" takes visitors through the different periods of American aviation history, complete with historic photographs, first-hand recollections, and more.

www.loc.gov/exhibits/treasures/wb-timeline.html
A timeline of Flight from 1000 BCE until 2000 AD.

www.nasm.si.edu/exhibitions/gal209/wrights.htm
An online Exhibition from the Smithsonian National Air and Space Museum about The Wright Brothers and The Invention of the Aerial Age. It tells the story of how Wilbur and Orville Wright invented the airplane—who they were, how they worked, and what they accomplished.

INDEX

ACKNOWLEDGMENTS

The publishers would like to thank: Graham Rich, Hazel Poole, and Elizabeth Wiggans
for their assistance and David Hobbs for his map of the world.

Picture research by Image Select.

Picture Credits: t=top, b=bottom, c=center, l=left, r=right, OFC=outside front cover,
AKG; 11br, 17br, 23cb, 29tr. Ann Ronan; 5br. Ann Ronan @ Image Select; 4/5b, 10cb, 10/11t, 12bl,
16tl, 18tl, 18bl, 37bl. Aviation Photographs International; 1 15br, 16/17b, 17cr, 22/23ct, 22/23cb,
28/29c, 30/31c, 31tr, 39cr, 41cr, 40/41c, 42tl. C.M. Scott; 22bl, 37c. Bibliotheque des Arts
Decoratifs, Paris/Archives Charmet/The Bridgeman Art Library: OFC. Colorific!; 30cl. Corbis-
Bettmann; 34bl. Francois Robineas, Dassault/Aviaplans; 19bl, 19br, 27tr, 32/33c, 33tr. Gamma; 40br.
Giraudon; 4bl, 7cr, 8tl, 15c, 16/17t. Greg Evans International Photo Library; 2tl, 6tl. Hulton
Deutsch Collection Ltd; 9tr, 31br, 33br. Hulton Getty; 16bl, 20tl, 25tr, 30tl, 36tr, 37cr. Image Select;
2 & 17br, 12/13b, 19tl, 30bl, 32bl, 34br, 35c, 43c. Mary Evans Picture Library; 5c, 7tr, 12tl, 13tl,
19tr, 21tr, 21cr, 26t, 27br, 28bl. Philip Jarrett; 6tl, 8bl, 9bl, 26bl, 26br, 26/27c, 32/33b. PIX; 4/5t,
6bl, 7br, 8/9t, 14bl, 37br, 38bl, 38/39 (main pic), 39tr. Planet Earth Pictures/Space Frontiers; 41br.
Quadrant Picture Library; 13ct, 12/13c, 14/15c, 15t, 21b, 32tl, 34/35c, 34/35t, 35tr, 35br, 34/35c,
36bl, 38tl, 41tl, 42tr. Retrograph Archive Ltd; 28bl, 29br, 29br. Salamander Picture Library; 20/21b,
30/31b, 43tl. Science and Society Picture Library; 6/7. Science Photo Library; 36c, 42c. Sutton
Libraries and Art Services; 22tl. Telegraph Colour Library; 34/35ct, 36/37t, 39cl. The Advertising
Archive; 28tl. UPI/Corbis; 25bl, 28/29t, 29bl.The Breitling Company; 40tl. The Smithsonian
Institution; 8/9c, 9cr, 11tr, 11cr, 12/13c, 12/13b, 14tl, 24/25c, 42/42b.

NOTE TO READERS

The website addresses are correct at the time of publishing. However, due to
the ever-changing nature of the Internet, websites and content may change.
Some websites can contain links that are unsuitable for children. The publisher
is not responsible for changes in content or website addresses. We advise
that Internet searches should be supervised by an adult.